CONTENTS

INTRODUCTION

Plastic pollution is an issue that has finally hit the mainstream agenda. From the public outcry at the shocking final episode of David Attenborough's *Blue Planet II* series to a recent commitment by the UK government to eliminate all plastic waste by 2042, the staggering scale of damage being done to our oceans is now broadly accepted as an environmental catastrophe we must take radical steps to avoid. But since we began manufacturing plastic on a mass scale in the 1950s, this by-product of the petrochemical industry has become so ubiquitous it now seems almost impossible to avoid.

Plastic is used in our clothing, food packets, electronics, bottles, paints and building materials. It's a vital component of our cars, phones and computers – even our homes and gardens. We wear it, watch it – even sleep on it. Plastic surrounds us all in one form or another, both day and night.

In fact, our reliance on plastic has grown to the point where humanity now produces its own weight in plastic every single year. That's 300 million tons (330 million US tons) – with a shocking 10–20 million tons (11–22 million US tons) of that ending up in the ocean. This is the equivalent of a truckload being dumped into the sea every single minute.

How does this plastic get into the sea? According to Greenpeace, roughly 80 per cent comes from the land – and by far the biggest source is plastic waste that's simply dropped or left behind on streets or in the countryside, which is carried by wind and rain into the sea.

The scale of the problem is so huge that the Ellen MacArthur Foundation – a British charity which campaigns to protect the oceans – predicts there will be more plastic than fish in the ocean by 2050.

The impact this has on our marine life is truly heartbreaking. Not only can creatures like dolphins and turtles become entangled in pieces of plastic, they can also mistake it for food. There have been cases of whales washed ashore with their stomachs full of plastic, leaving no space for food. Studies have revealed that up to 90 per cent of seabirds have plastic in their digestive systems and micro-plastics (broken-down plastic particles which are eaten by filter feeders such as plankton, then by fish and then by humans) have been found in table salt, tap water and beer. Even closer to home, our landfills continue to overflow with plastic, some of which has been around for decades.

Plastic was originally hailed as a miracle product, but now we know the downsides to this incredibly versatile material – the problem is, plastic never

HOW TO GO
PLASTIC FREE

ECO TIPS FOR BUSY PEOPLE

CAROLINE JONES

THIS IS A CARLTON BOOK

This book is 100 per cent plastic-free and biodegradable.

Published in 2018 by Carlton Books
An imprint of the Carlton Publishing Group
20 Mortimer Street
London W1T 3JW

A CIP catalogue for this book is available from the British Library.

ISBN 978-1-78739-196-3

Printed in China

10 9 8 7 6 5 4 3 2 1

goes away. Every single piece of plastic ever created still exists – even if it's the 10 per cent that is broken down and recycled for secondary use. This is a fact that should shock us all into action.

With everyday life so dependent on a vast variety of plastic products, making the shift to a life without plastic can feel like a real challenge. However, the good news is, there are many simple ways to cut down on plastic use. Often, it's just a case of taking a moment to stop and question whether there is another option or a different way.

You may feel using plastic is inescapable, but this book is here to help make the transition away from plastic easy, step-by-step. Packed with simple ways to start reducing your plastic use – today – this book is here to help you find practical alternatives in all areas of your life, whatever your budget.

From buying loose fruit and vegetables to rethinking your cleaning products, these simple tips will help you find safe, reusable and affordable alternatives while revealing various health, cost and waste benefits, with ideas for responsible recycling and on how to deal with the existing plastic in your home – including ingenious ideas for upcycling instead of simply throwing away. Think of it as the ultimate beginner's guide to living plastic free.

And if you think that one person using less plastic won't save the world, remember this is how all positive change begins. Most governments and manufacturing companies are now taking this issue seriously, but with change on that scale likely to be slow, we all ultimately share the responsibility to end plastic pollution now.

We also have enormous collective power through the choices we make as consumers. Together, we can create demand for plastic-free products and packaging alternatives simply by shopping differently.

The important thing is to take the first step. Eradicating plastic will not happen overnight and it's easy to be overwhelmed by all of the changes you could potentially make. But just making one change a week will eventually add up to a big difference. Pick some easy swaps first to motivate yourself, or focus on the ideas that will make the biggest impact. For example, if you have a daily single-use plastic water bottle habit you can cut that out immediately and resolve to drink tap water in a reusable bottle instead.

Once you do make a personal commitment, you can increase the impact of your own choices by simply talking to others, including friends and family, about why you now prefer to buy products with less plastic. In this way, one person inspires another and before long a ripple becomes a wave of change that can remake our world for the better – for our own future and for many generations to come.

GETTING STARTED

If living with lower levels of plastic was easy, everyone would be doing it. We may all accept that plastic is harming the environment, but it's so prolific that avoiding it can be tough. The key is to do it gradually, introducing a few changes at a time. Read on to kick-start your transition to plastic-free living.

#1
FORMING NEW HABITS

Living without plastic is a big change for anyone. To make any change stick, it needs to become a habit. Habits form naturally when we repeat a new behaviour a certain number of times. Conscious choices become automatic, allowing you to make a behaviour part of your routine and continue it for the longer term. Right now, most of us have a pretty ingrained habit of using plastic multiple times a day. The trick is to break these old habits and replace them with new, greener ones. If you've ever tried before to make – and keep – a New Year's resolution or start a new diet, you'll know that if you go in with an all-or-nothing attitude, your attempt is usually doomed. Just like cutting out all chocolate is impossible for most of us to keep up forever, banning all plastic straight away isn't realistically achievable. This kind of blanket ban only sets you up for backsliding and ultimate failure, which means the new habit won't have enough time to form and you'll end up going back to your old plastic-using ways in no time.

So it's important to realize you should not attempt to go 100 per cent plastic-free immediately. The recipe for success is to take it slowly, one step at a time. Start with the easiest plastic items to find substitutes for, then build up from there. This will help you create a plastic-free mindset, and you won't feel overwhelmed. Here are some ways to get started…

#2
DON'T THROW ALL YOUR PLASTIC OUT AT ONCE!

When you decide to go plastic-free it can be tempting to have a complete purge and clear your home of everything that contains plastic. However, don't forget all the plastic you throw out will create a huge amount of waste, probably ending up in a landfill or harming the environment somewhere. A better idea is to take the time to sort and select plastic items for charity donation, where they can be reused if in good condition. Or if an item in your home is currently being put to good use, then it might be better off staying where it is for now. The real decisive shift is committing to not buying any new plastic products. Once you stop adding plastic to your home you can gradually discover how to replace the items you already have, along with the best way to dispose of things responsibly.

#3
GET SUPPORT

Plastic-free living is a fast-growing movement gathering members and momentum all around the world, which means there are bound to be others in your local area embarking on the same journey. So look online for local forums and Facebook groups based near you. Here you can ask questions, find information on the best local places to buy plastic-free alternatives and share your own tips on reducing plastic. You can even vent frustrations on any part of plastic-free living you're finding tough. And like any new challenge, you'll find it easier to stay motivated if you've got like-minded people at the click of a button to offer chat and support.

#4

START CAMPAIGNING

As well as making simple swaps at home, there are a number of campaigns you can get involved with to help create real change. This will also immerse you more completely in the plastic-free movement. A Plastic Planet is a grassroots campaign urging supermarkets to install plastic-free aisles, and Friends of the Earth is currently petitioning governments everywhere to look at how they're handling the plastic pollution crisis.

#5

SAY NO TO SINGLE
USE PLASTICS – FOR GOOD

Your first change for the better should be to stop using single-use plastics. Often in the form of food packaging, this is any plastic used just once and then thrown away or recycled. It's so convenient, single-use plastic has seeped into every corner of our lives, but the negative impact it has on the environment is so immense we need to break this reliance.

For example, it's become normal for many people to buy a drink in a plastic bottle and a plastic wrapped sandwich every lunchtime, then carry them out of the shop in a plastic bag – all of which are used for just a couple of minutes before being discarded forever.

Yet the huge amount of plastic needed to supply this takeaway lunch habit is terrifying. Even if only 15 per cent of the world did this daily throughout their working lives that's over 2,400 billion batches of discarded lunchtime plastic. It's impossible to escape the consequences of throwing away such vast quantities of a material that takes hundreds of years to break down. And while some single-use plastics items such as plastic bottles can be recycled, many can't. Which makes them the worst form of plastic in use – hands down.

So if there is a significant change to sign up to right away, it's ditching single-use plastic that can't be recycled.

HERE ARE THE TOP 10 WORST SINGLE-USE PLASTICS OFFENDERS:

1. Crisp packets

2. Wet wipes

3. Sandwich packaging

4. Sauce sachets

5. Ready-meal trays

6. Pet food pouches

7. Cotton buds

8. Plant pots

9. Plastic drinking straws

10. "Foilized" (metallic) wrapping paper

EATING & DRINKING

Food and drink is probably the area of our life in which we encounter the most unnecessary plastic. But the good news is, with a few smart changes, you can cut down your consumption significantly – and make a sizeable environmental difference in the process.

SHOPPING

It may take a little planning to use less plastic when you shop, but fear not, it can be done.

#6

SWITCH TO REUSABLE SHOPPING BAGS

Plastic bags have been on the environmental hit list for many years now and yet about 1 million plastic bags are still used every minute worldwide, with every single one taking up to 1,000 years to degrade.

If you haven't yet made the switch, simply take three or four reusable bags with you whenever you go shopping. This will immediately end your plastic bag waste. Simple canvas "bag for life" totes are readily and cheaply available and can be put through the washing machine when dirty. Made from cotton, they are also biodegradable.

Remembering to take your canvas bags can sometimes be a problem, which is why a great alternative is to buy a couple of compressible bags (found easily online), which scrunch up to almost nothing and are virtually weightless. Keeping these permanently in your jacket pocket or handbag means you'll never be caught out again. And remember, don't just use these bags for groceries – use them to carry everything you buy, from clothes to electronics and toiletries.

#7

SELL BACK OLD PLASTIC BAGS!

Some supermarkets will actually pay to take used plastic bags off your hands when you shop online, paying you a small amount for each bag you hand to the driver when your order is delivered. The supermarket will usually deduct the total value of the bags from the cost of your current order or your next order, depending on when you hand them back. Some supermarkets will even accept bags from any rival, so you can happily recycle all your plastic bags in one go. Any returned bags are then recycled into new ones, which means you've reduced your plastic waste and saved money in one go!

#8

STOP BUYING BOTTLED WATER

This simple but important measure is one you can start immediately. Even if you plan to recycle your plastic drinks bottle, enormous amounts of energy and resources have still been used to extract, bottle and ship it around the world. Bottled water produces 1.5 million tons (1.68 million US tons) of plastic waste per year, and these bottles also require 47 million gallons (77 million US gallons) of oil to produce, according to Food & Water Watch. The US is addicted to bottled water, spending an astonishing $12 billion a year on it. According to plastic recycling charity Recoup Recycling, the UK alone uses 13 billion plastic bottles each year, so it's fair to say they're a significant source of plastic waste.

#9

SWITCH TO TAP WATER

Many countries around the world now have drinking water available from the tap. The water in the UK and USA is some of the cleanest and safest in the world. You can filter it if you prefer the taste – either with a standard filter jug or to go completely plastic-free, try charcoal. Charcoal is an extremely porous material that absorbs and holds a wide range of harmful contaminants. Many companies, including Black+Blum, sell an affordable stick that you simply place in a water jug or stainless steel bottle, where it will filter the water for you.

#10
ADD SOME BUBBLES

If you love sparkling water, invest in a SodaStream, the 1980s fizzy favourite that has recently been repositioned as an eco-product. You can make as much carbonated water as you like without having to throw away a single bottle. The more expensive models even come with glass bottles to store the water in. Each gas canister, which can be refilled, makes up to 60 litres (16 US gallons) of water very affordably. The leading sparkling water brand would cost you around five times the price of a 1-litre (33 oz) bottle you produced at home.

#11
SAY NO TO STRAWS

One of the top 10 worst plastic waste offenders, the 70 million plastic straws estimated to end up in landfills each year aren't recycled for the simple reason that they are too small to be picked out during the separating process. The UK government has already announced plans to ban them by 2019 and across the US, New York City, California and Hawaii have ban legislation in the works, but you can keep them out of the landfill now by refusing to buy them or to use them when you're out. If you or the kids still want to use a straw to drink with, try recyclable paper straws, or better still, many retailers now sell reusable stainless steel or glass drinking straws.

#12
SKIP CRISPS

Unbelievably, there is currently no plastic-free crisp packaging widely available from any brand. Although the inside of a crisps packet is shiny and looks like foil, it is in fact a metallized plastic film. Indeed, most crisp packets consist of multiple layers of different plastics, including an outer layer, inside layer and sealant.

While this ensures the packaging is lightweight and keeps the contents fresh, the mixture of materials involved makes crisp packets a nightmare when it comes to plastic pollution. And because crisp packets are currently non-recyclable, they all end up in a landfill.

Sadly, the kind of crisps that come in a cardboard tube aren't much better either, as they tend to have a metal lining and plastic lid, making them "mixed material" and therefore very difficult to recycle. This means crisp-lovers everywhere need to call upon manufacturers to change their packets to materials which are easily recyclable – or even better, a non-plastic environmentally-friendly material. In the meantime, you can always make tasty crisps at home.

#13
RECIPE: HOMEMADE CRISPS

This easy recipe means you can still enjoy crisps without using plastic.

Ingredients
Serves: 4
1 tablespoon vegetable oil
1 washed potato, sliced paper-thin
(peeling isn't necessary but you can if you prefer)
½ teaspoon salt, or to taste

To make:
Pour the vegetable oil into a bowl – add the potato slices and toss
to evenly coat with oil. Then lightly coat a large dinner plate with
oil and arrange the potato slices in a single layer on the plate.
Cook in the microwave for three to five minutes, or until lightly
browned (if not browned, they will not become crisp). Times will
vary depending on your microwave power. Remove from the
plate and toss with salt (you can add other seasonings to taste
such as paprika, garlic powder or pepper). Leave to cool. Repeat
the process with the remaining potato slices.

#14
BUY LOOSE, BUY LESS

Buying loose fruit and veg not only cuts down on plastic use, it also reduces food waste by encouraging you to buy only the amount you actually need for that week. You're usually better off going to larger supermarkets, farmers' markets or greengrocer's for more choice when it comes to unpackaged produce – and don't forget to bring your own reusable bags. You may even save some money too, as an investigation by UK website Money Saving Expert found many items – including mushrooms, apples, courgettes, broccoli and bananas – were significantly cheaper to buy loose rather than pre-packed when purchased at the same shop. Similarly, you can buy cheese and meat at deli counters, using your own reusable containers to transport home.

#15
CHANGE HOW YOU BUY MILK

Supermarket milk comes in plastic bottles which, while recyclable, are only single-use, so energy inefficient. Shops do sell smaller amounts of milk in cardboard containers, which may seem like a good option at first, but these cartons are actually coated inside and out with plastic, making them tough to recycle. This means your best bet is to go old school and start using a milkman – as the majority of people did until around 30 years ago. Most areas still have dairies that deliver locally and provide milk in returnable, reusable glass bottles.

#16

BUY NON-PERISHABLES IN BULK

Buying large amounts in one go not only cuts down on unnecessary plastic and packaging, it also works out much cheaper in the long run. But it does require a little more planning, and creating adequate space for storage. The trick is to bulk buy non-perishables that will store happily for months. This covers a range of foods, including large bottles of oil, bags of rice, lentils and dried beans, along with pasta and cereals. Non-perishables also include bottled toiletries, pet food and toilet rolls.

#17
TRY LARGER SUPERMARKETS TO FIND BIGGER SIZES OF PRODUCTS

Many health food stores, such as Planet Organic and Whole Foods UK, also sell bulk grains like rice, nuts, cereal and granola, and opting to fill a reusable bag or container with these items will save both money and unnecessary packaging. Stores have various methods for deducting the container weight, so simply check with customer service before filling yours.

#18
BUY TOILET PAPER WITHOUT PLASTIC PACKAGING

The humble loo roll is one area in which it's hard to go plastic-free, as it's almost impossible to find shop-bought toilet paper that doesn't come wrapped in plastic. So your only real option is to order it online. Brands Ecoleaf and Greencane use fully compostable packaging, while Cheeky Panda offers toilet paper that can be ordered in bulk with zero packaging – just the cardboard box it travels in.

#19
DON'T BUY JUICE

Instead of buying juice in plastic bottles or the common cartons, like Tetra Pak, which have plastic coatings, and are therefore even more difficult to recycle, make your own freshly squeezed juice. The greenest options are to invest in a juicer with as few plastic parts as possible, or to buy one secondhand. Cheaper still, you could always buy a simple stainless-steel hand juicer and do it the old-fashioned way. Not only will home juicing cut down on plastic waste, it's also better for you because being fresher means you'll consume higher levels of health-boosting vitamins and antioxidants compared to juice that's travelled thousands of miles and sat on a supermarket shelf for some time.

#20

THINK ABOUT HOW YOU BUY MEAT

Another group of products that ranked high on the top 10 worst plastic offenders list was the black plastic trays most shops tend to use for meat. Because of the black pigment used in the tray, they cannot be picked up by infrared technology at material recycling facilities and end up in landfill. A better alternative is to buy meat from the meat counter at the supermarket or deli or, better still, from your local butcher who will likely sell locally reared produce. Take your own brown paper and ask that it's wrapped up in that for you, rather than the plastic wrapping that tends to be used.

#21

AVOID FROZEN FOODS

Frozen foods offer convenience, but with a huge amount of plastic packaging thrown in. Even so-called eco-friendly packaged items made from cardboard are often coated in a thin layer of plastic. While giving up frozen food can be difficult, there are benefits besides the obvious environmental ones – you'll end up eating fewer processed foods and avoiding any chemicals in their plastic packaging.

#22
GET A COFFEE CONSCIENCE

At home the capsules used in popular single-serve coffee machines contain plastic and are notoriously bad for the environment. One option is to source biodegradable options, such as Halo, who make compostable pods compatible with most popular machines. But generally speaking, loose coffee is the greenest way to go – either ground or whole beans. This means seeking out smaller, independent coffee shops and delis in your area, and taking your own jar or tin to fill up.

#23
SWITCH TO LOOSE TEA

Did you know that the 165 million teabags thrown away every day in the UK contain plastic? Polypropylene is added to each paper teabag during manufacture to help heat-seal them so they don't come open in the box or your cup of tea. This means that nearly all of the teabags we buy aren't 100 per cent biodegradable – so the bags you might be composting could be leaving tiny bits of microplastic in the soil. The safest bet is to choose loose-leaf tea wherever possible and brew it in a stainless-steel tea ball, or you could just use an old-fashioned teapot and metal hand strainer.

#24
BUY REFILLS WHERE POSSIBLE

Simple but effective. Buying refills of products such as air freshener, liquid soap, coffee, herbs and spices saves money as well as cutting down on plastic waste in terms of lids, bottles and so on. But be careful: most refills will still result in some plastic waste, so it's always worth comparing just how recyclable the packaging is compared to that of the original.

#25

CHOOSE BRANDS WITH
A GOOD TRACK RECORD

Companies such as Coca-Cola, Marks & Spencer and Unilever are pioneers in improving the sustainability of their products and ensuring their packaging can be recycled once used. Read up online on what your favourite brands are doing and what similar brands are doing – then take your business to the companies that have the most progressive attitude to plastics.

#26
AVOID FOIL POUCHES

Another member of the top 10 worst waste list. Pouches used for soups, pet food, baby food and some juice drinks use two types of plastic with a foil layer on the inside, making them practically unrecyclable. The only current method for recycling requires them to be entirely separated from other items, then put through a complicated process using microwaves to cook off all of the different materials at their respective boiling points. Needless to say, that's very expensive and uses up a lot of energy, so generally isn't possible. While they may be convenient, these pouches have often replaced something altogether easier to recycle – the humble aluminium food can and drinks tin. Tins and cans are easily picked out with magnets, melted down and reused an almost unlimited number of times.

#27
MAKE YOUR OWN CONDIMENTS

Those squeezy plastic bottles your favourite sauces come in might or might not be recyclable – depending on the type of plastic they're made from. Those with "1" stamped on the bottom are made from PET (polyethylene terephthalate) which can usually be recycled through normal home collection schemes. However, do wash them out thoroughly as research has found that leftover sauce means not all squeezy bottles make it through the sorting process due to "contamination" and so may still end up in landfill. Many other plastic squeezy bottles are made from LDPE (low density polyethylene) plastic and have "4" on the base, which is not currently collected or recycled. So why not make your own condiments? If you dedicate a whole day to it, you could produce enough to last the entire year! The best time to make ketchup is when tomatoes are at their peak in the late summer. Items such as chocolate sauce, mustard and mayonnaise are also quick and simple to make once you get the hang of them. Everything can be kept in sterilized and sealed glass jars, for months if unopened.

#28
HOMEMADE KETCHUP RECIPE

Ingredients
200g (1 cup) of any tomatoes, chopped
2 teaspoons light brown sugar
1 tablespoon vinegar
1 teaspoon salt
1 teaspoon paprika
1 teaspoon Worcestershire sauce

To make:
Place all the ingredients in a saucepan on a medium-high heat and
bring to the boil, stirring occasionally. Reduce the heat and let simmer
gently for 10 minutes. Then remove from heat and allow to cool for
5 minutes. Finally, whiz in a blender or food processor until smooth,
then sieve into a bowl. After opening, you can store in an airtight
glass jar in the fridge for up to four weeks.

#29
LEAVE PLASTIC AT THE SUPERMARKET

If you're feeling brave and want to make a stand, then next time you're doing your supermarket shop, Greenpeace advise taking some of the plastic packaging you don't want off the products you do want, and leaving it at the checkout. It might sound scary, but you're well within your rights to do it – and you're actually helping the supermarket to understand what their customers really want. It's also worth writing to the most senior management team of your closest supermarket to lobby for less plastic packaging.

#30
AVOID ONLINE SHOPPING THAT CREATES PLASTIC WASTE

Buying online – whether it's food, furniture or other items – can create a real plastic problem, with companies using non-recyclable, plastic-based packaging from outer envelopes to bubble wrap, polystyrene padding to chips. To avoid this completely it's well worth looking first to see if you can find these items at a local shop rather than online. Many bigger shops now offer price-matching to internet sites if you say that it is available cheaper online.

#31
BUY SECOND-HAND OVER NEW

Another way to avoid delivery materials is to see if you can get them second-hand, or even borrow from a friend as needed. A good first stop is to check local "buy, sell or swap" Facebook groups and forums, followed by online auction sites such as eBay to see if you can get what you need there. Many have the option of setting up an email alert as soon as someone puts up a new ad for a specific product you're looking for. Sellers on second-hand websites are often more willing to send a package with very little packaging and no plastic – wrapping it in old newspaper, for example. Just send a message to the seller to ask whether it is possible to send the item without any plastic and in a reused box or just a plain paper envelope, explaining that you're trying to use less plastic.

#32

ASK SHOPS FOR PLASTIC-FREE SHIPPING

If an item is only available online, it's always worth sending a message to the shop before you place an order to ask whether it is possible to ship the package without using plastic. Again, explain why. Set up a standard message that you can reuse to save time. It's also worth adding you'd appreciate them choosing the smallest, appropriately sized packing box, so there isn't lots of space that needs filling up with plastic chips or other padding to protect the product. Bigger online shops can be less flexible, so it's worth trying smaller ones. By sending an email before placing an order you're not only preventing plastic waste, you're sending a very clear message to the shop that you – and other consumers – don't want to receive lots of plastic packaging material. Long-term, this will help encourage shops to change their packaging habits to keep customers happy.

#33
BEWARE OF "BIODEGRADABLE" PACKING MATERIAL

Some shops write in their packaging policy that they substitute normal plastic with biodegradable plastic. While getting a package filled with packing chips that can break down is certainly better, it's worth noting that biodegradable plastic doesn't break down in a garden composter. Compostable plastic needs industrial composting facility conditions to decompose. Even then, plastic will still not break down 100 per cent, so recyclable paper is still always a better choice.

#34
RETHINK HOW YOU STORE FOOD

Changing your food storage means switching resealable plastic
tubs for something more eco-friendly. Good alternatives for storing
leftovers in the fridge include glass, such as Mason or Kilner jars or
Pyrex containers. When it comes to freezing foods in glass, the trick
is not to completely fill the container as the food will expand inside,
and then to thaw it slowly at room temperature to avoid breakages.
If you run out of jars at home, simply store leftovers in bowls with
saucers on top instead of foil or clingfilm. Grease-proof paper is
also a greener alternative to plastic bags when it comes to wrapping
small amounts of food.

#35
REUSE GLASS CONTAINERS

A huge variety of prepared foods still come in glass jars, including pasta sauce, peanut butter, salsa and jam to name just a few. Instead of throwing the empties away or recycling them, wash and reuse the jars to store food or as shopping containers when you're buying bulk foods. If you have plastic containers left over from yogurt, butter or other food, don't throw them out either. Using them to store other food is better than them ending up in landfill.

#36
GIVE PLASTIC FOOD WRAP THE COLD SHOULDER

This stretchy, clear food wrap is generally made from polyvinyl chloride (PVC), a material that is not only single-use and totally non-recyclable, it's also been suggested it could be harmful to human health. Beeswax and soy wax wraps are great reusable, biodegradable alternatives to clingfilm and are now widely available. Made from cotton, wax and resin, these wraps can be moulded around containers and food to keep it fresh. They can also be washed, dried and reused for up to a year and, once spent, many can be composted. Wraps cost from around the price of a whole roll of plastic food wrap to double that, so they don't come cheap. But depending on how much clingfilm you get through, they could help you save – use a wrap pack for a year and it should pay for itself.

#37
GO GADGET FREE, WHERE POSSIBLE

There are so many fancy kitchen gadgets these days, each promising to make light work of having to chop, mix, steam and slice. Unfortunately, nearly all such gadgets have plastic parts, meaning it's all too easy to accumulate a host of plastic-based tools you'll probably rarely use. Ask yourself if you really need another gadget and whether you already have an item that will do a similar job. Not only are you being kind to the environment, you'll be grateful for the extra drawer and cupboard space in the long run. If a gadget is essential, look on eBay or local "buy, sell and swap" forums for second-hand ones in good condition.

IS PLASTIC HARMING OUR HEALTH?

Whether plastic poses health dangers to people has been a hot topic of debate for the past 20 years. At a UK workshop in 2018, organized by the marine group Common Sea and attended by 30 leading scientists and doctors, it was agreed unanimously that plastic is now in everything we eat, drink and breathe – and therefore constitutes a significant threat to human health.

The concern is that if we can swallow and breathe in these tiny micro-plastic particles, they could enter the bloodstream, lungs and, for nursing mums, their breast milk. Once inside the body, many plastics are suspected to be both carcinogenic and hormone-disrupting. Experts agree that much more research is needed to uncover exactly how these tiny fragments of plastic could affect the body. But while the evidence grows, this is yet another argument to reduce your exposure to plastic.

SHOULD BPA BE BANNED?

Bisphenol A – also known as BPA – a material widely added to food and drink packaging to create a special form of robust polycarbonate plastic, is of particular concern to health experts. First created in 1891, it's now one of the most commonly produced chemicals in the world, with an estimated 2.5 million tons (2.8 million US tons) generated every year.

The main health concern is that BPA can be ingested or absorbed through skin contact, meaning that we are regularly exposed to the chemical as it leaches out of packaging into our food and drink. One study by the University of Exeter in 2018 found that more than 80 per cent of teenagers have BPA in their bodies. But just how dangerous is it?

Well, once in the human body, BPA mimics the action of the hormone oestrogen and could therefore disrupt the entire hormone system. Over the past 20 years various studies have linked BPA to a variety of adverse health effects, including a higher risk of infertility, breast cancer and diabetes. Particular concern has been raised over the possible impact on babies and young children.

As a result, the US Food and Drug Administration has banned BPA use in baby bottles and cups, while France has completely banned the use of BPA in any packaging that comes into contact with food.

Until the UK government enforces such a ban, reducing overall use of plastics will help limit your exposure. But if you do have to buy any plastic-wrapped food items or containers, look out for a "BPA-free" label, which many brands now have.

EATING ON THE MOVE

Our ever-expanding appetite for food on the go is one of the biggest sources of plastic waste, and a problem in need of radical solutions.

#38

SEARCH OUT NON-PLASTIC DINNERWARE

Plastic has become the material of choice for feeding young children and for eating outdoors. By far the worst culprits are the single-use type plates made from non-recyclable polystyrene, which generally end up in a landfill or worse in the ocean, where they can harm marine wildlife. Most reusable child plates and cups are made from polypropylene, a material that can be recycled in theory, but not in practice as most UK councils don't include it among their acceptable household recycling items. As a result, kids' cups and plates most often end up – you've guessed it – in a landfill, where polypropylene will take up to 400 years to breakdown.

Melamine is another popular material for single-use dinnerware, but this can't be melted down for recycling, unlike other plastics, and again it's not accepted as part of UK household recycling schemes – only at specialist centres.

So your best eco bet is to seek out some of the hard-wearing plate and cup ranges made from bamboo, corn or sugar cane. These all have a nice solid feel, tend to come in a range of bright colours and some can be used in the microwave before being cleaned in the dishwasher. Better still, they're made from fast-growing, renewable plant materials and are therefore fully biodegradable and/or compostable. Searching online or in your nearest organic shop is your best bet to source them. Good brands to look out for include Zuperzozial and Living Eco Dining.

#39
READYMADE SANDWICHES

Brits alone spent £8 billion ($10.5 billion) on ready-made sandwiches in 2017 and 50 per cent of Americans eat a sandwich every day – but the standard sandwich packaging is a particular problem for recycling plants. Not only are the triangular containers mostly made from plastic laminated card – which makes separating plastic layers from paper ones extremely difficult – they also have a see-through window made from an entirely different type of plastic. Indeed, while there has been a lot of talk about imposing a "latte-levy" to put people off using disposable coffee cups, environmental experts say it would be just as vital to impose a sandwich pack levy too. Sandwich packaging is, in fact, an area where the food industry is going backwards when it comes to responsible plastic use. Older containers, often made entirely from clear plastic, were far simpler to recycle, but these days the fashion for fancier packets made from several different materials makes recycling much tougher.

#40
GIVE UP GUM

Chewing gum was originally made from tree sap called chicle, a natural rubber from plants. But when scientists created synthetic rubber, polyethylene and polyvinyl acetate began to replace chicle in many brands of gum. But it's hard to know exactly which brands contain what as manufacturers only need to list the rather vague term "gum base" in the list of ingredients, and aren't required to go into any more detail on what that is made from.

But there's a pretty good chance you will be chewing on plastic, so while it is possible to recycle gum, it may be best to skip it – and its plastic packaging – altogether.

#41

INVEST IN A REUSABLE WATER BOTTLE

Just because you've now stopped buying single-use plastic water bottles, it doesn't mean you have to stop taking water out and about with you. You simply need to buy a reusable container. Obviously, plastic is out, and glass can feel both heavy and fragile, so the latest stainless steel bottles are an ideal choice – they're lightweight and keep water cool and fresh tasting.

Plus, you'll be saving money. Reusable water bottle prices start from around 10 times the cost of a standard branded bottle of mineral water. So within 10 uses, your bottle will have paid for itself.

#42
REFILL FREE

Run out of water when you're out? Don't succumb and buy a bottle from the shop. Why not see if you can refill free instead? There are now several apps, around the world, which can help you find cafés, restaurants, shops and hotels which will let you do this even if you're not a customer. Tapwater.org is a not-for-profit organization that promotes the drinking of tap water and aims to reduce the use of bottled water. Enter your location on their app to find "refilling stations" near you. Many café and hotel chains – including Costa and Premier Inn – have also joined the Water UK campaign, which means you can use their facilities to refill a water bottle without being a paying customer. The initiative aims to enable people to refill their water free in tens of thousands of places by 2021.

#43
CARRY YOUR CUP

When it comes to your shop-bought flat white, investing in your own reusable cup will not only reduce your plastic use, it can also save you some money. Several high street coffee chains now offer a discount on coffee if you bring your own cup. Good choices are those made from steel or natural bamboo fibre. Both are fully dishwasher-safe and have no nasty plastic aftertaste.

#44
CARRY CUTLERY WITH YOU

It's time to say goodbye to disposable plastic chopsticks, knives, spoons and forks for good, as even the recyclable ones require a lot of resources to make and recycle. If you take your lunch to work or you know your favourite restaurant only has plasticware, start keeping a set of clean utensils in your bag!

#45
PACK LUNCH THE RIGHT WAY

There are many reasons to take your own lunch to work, to school or to the park, but one of the most compelling arguments is that buying takeaway lunch inevitably involves lots of single-use plastic packaging that you can completely avoid by bringing your own food. But a packed lunch does require planning to ensure your lunchbox doesn't end up full of disposable plastic containers and sandwich bags. First of all, ditch bags and put snacks inside any small, reusable containers you have at home. You can also buy foods such as yogurt in bulk and simply put a lunch-sized portion in a reusable tub. When it comes to a plastic-free lunchbox itself, look out for stainless steel bento boxes or those made from bamboo.

#46

SIT DOWN FOR A PROPER MEAL

Our obsession with eating on the go or food delivery is a relatively recent development. The simplest way to avoid disposable takeout boxes is to take the time to make a special meal at home or dine in properly at local restaurants, savouring both the food and the company.

TAKEAWAYS AND RESTAURANTS

Unfortunately, most takeaway packaging isn't recyclable, so the box that was in your hands for 10 minutes on Friday night could end up in the ocean forever (see p.56). Plus, even those boxes that can be thrown into general recycling can't be sorted for reuse if they have any food residue on them that can't be rinsed off.

#47

SHUN THE SACHET SAUCE

Those little packets of ketchup and mustard found at fast food restaurants and takeaways present a double whammy of bad news for recycling centres. Not only are they too small to sort easily, they're also made from multiple materials: a plastic outer layer with a lining made of foil or a different plastic. Avoid the waste by saucing your food at home – or even bringing a small glass container of your favourite sauce with you.

WHAT HAPPENS TO YOUR TAKEAWAY BOX?

Imagine your takeaway box has made its way to
sea via a network of rivers, moving with the currents
until it reaches the deep ocean. At this stage, it's
still a megaplastic (item of plastic bigger than 10
cm (4in)). These plastics have been manufactured to
resist age and not break down easily. Over time, with
the pounding of the waves, they will however slowly
degrade and break down into macroplastics (2.5 cm
to 10 cm (1–4 in)), mesoplastics (5 mm to 2.5 cm
($^{13}/_{64}$ to 4 in)), microplastics (smaller than 5 mm ($^{13}/_{64}$
in)) and sometimes even into nano plastic particles
(the equivalent of around $^1/_{70}$ of the width of a human
hair). But if your ex-takeaway box has over time been
broken into millions of pieces, this is actually the point
at which it becomes the most dangerous – these tiny
particles can be eaten by marine life, releasing toxic
chemicals into their metabolism and permanently
entering the food chain.

#48
BRING YOUR OWN CONTAINER

Whether you're picking up a takeaway or bringing home restaurant leftovers, be prepared by packing your own reusable containers. If you're placing an order over the phone, ask if you can get the food placed in your own container. Most restaurants shouldn't have a problem with this.

#49
USE PESTER POWER

Buy local and get to know the staff in your favourite shops and food and drink establishments, so you feel able to request they provide sustainable alternatives to "disposable" plastics – for instance, reusable cutlery that can be washed, or FSC (wood sourced from renewable forests), wooden disposable cutlery and 100 per cent paper-cardboard takeaway boxes.

GREENER
HOME LIFE

A huge amount of plastic waste piles up at home. Our desire for easy ways to look good, clean and take care of our kids has resulted in plastic infiltrating every area of domestic life. The good news is with a wealth of greener products now available, it's easier than ever to cut your home plastic footprint.

BEAUTY & GROOMING

How many different plastic bottles do you have in your bathroom? Even if you only have five products that you replace monthly, that can easily add up to 60 plastic bottles a year per family member. Here's how to cut down.

#50
STREAMLINE YOUR REGIME

Less is more! Perhaps the simplest way to cut down on plastics in the bathroom is to use fewer products. Are your shelves lined with different creams, gels and potions – many of which you never use? Think about what products you can do without and those that could work harder – do you really need a separate face wash, shower gel and hand soap, or could one good-quality soap do the job? By gradually reducing the number of items that you use, and just sticking with the essentials, you can save time, money, and of course the plastic that they come in.

#51
BUY IN BULK

If you have the space, buying in bulk will save you money and reduce your packaging consumption. UK-based brand Faith in Nature is an award-winning organic, vegan beauty company that uses 100 per cent PET (completely recyclable) recycled plastic in all its packaging. You can buy both shampoo and conditioners in huge 5-litre bottles which will last anyone a long time. Dr Bronner's soap for face, body and hair meanwhile, has a cult following and is also available in up to 5-litre (1.3 US gallons) recycled plastic bottles. Simply decant into smaller glass bottles to store in your shower or to take travelling.

#52

USE RECYCLED OR RECYCLABLE PACKAGING

The next easiest switch you can make is avoiding products housed in plastic and instead choose brands with packaging that can be recycled or reused, such as glass. Luxury brands like Aesop, Tata Harper and Kjaer Weis are great go-tos when it comes to both gorgeous products and great eco-credentials. Mid-priced Neal's Yard Remedies and Aveda are beauty companies that use 100 per cent recycled plastic in their packaging and also come in big sizes.

#53
TRY BEAUTY IN A TIN!

Even better than recyclable plastic packaging is to opt for beauty products that miss out plastics altogether. Health food stores and online eco stores now sell skincare brands such as ila and White Rabbit, which make sunscreen, lip creams and other products in recyclable aluminium tins. Make-up brands including Zao have created blushers, eyeshadows and other products housed in sustainable bamboo packaging with an innovative refill system to reduce plastic waste. Check out the beauty counter in your local health food store.

#54
STOP USING FACE WIPES

Standard wet cleansing wipes, with all their throwaway ease, are not biodegradable and cause huge problems in landfills and our oceans. Many people toss them in the recycling bin, thinking they're going to be recyclable, but this isn't usually the case. They're basically a woven plastic, designed to stay moist without ever rotting or breaking down. As a greener alternative, remove make-up using your normal cleanser and either a cotton flannel or an eco-friendly konjac sponge, made from natural plant fibre. You can also look out for eco beauty companies selling biodegradable or compostable wipes, e.g. Free From Wish-a-Wash Wet Wipes.

#55

SWAP SHOWER GEL FOR SOAP

Another easy win. Bars of soap generally last longer, so work out cheaper. You can buy a bar of standard soap for half the price of the same brand equivalent shower gel. Plus, soaps generally use far less plastic packaging and can often be bought with no packaging at all.

#56

TRY A SHAMPOO BAR

Solid shampoos in bar form have become hugely popular among beauty bloggers in the last few years. They boast zero packaging and zero waste, often coming loose or wrapped in plastic-free paper, making them a far greener choice than any bottle of shampoo. Being more concentrated than liquid shampoo, less product is needed per wash, making it a very cost-effective purchase too. Beauty brand Lush produces a large range of colourful shampoo bars for all hair types, and claims that by creating this solid alternative it has saved almost six million plastic bottles per year.

#57

WATCH OUT FOR MICROBEADS

Until January 2018, many UK face and body scrubs and some toothpastes contained plastic microbeads. But these small spheres, designed to help with exfoliation and then be washed away, were being carried into the oceans, where they don't break down and end up being eaten by fish – effectively putting toxic chemicals into the food chain. While the ban is good news, microbeads are still permitted in non rinse-off products such as lipstick and sun creams, so you should carefully check ingredients lists and stick to eco-friendly brands which don't use them in anything.

#58
SWITCH SANITARY PRODUCTS

In one woman's lifetime she will use an average of 12,000–16,000 disposable feminine hygiene products, of which 90 per cent contain plastic materials. A plastic pad or applicator alone can take 100 years to degrade. In the UK, more than three billion sanitary items are bought every year, so just by ensuring your time of the month is plastic free, you could make a real difference. Alternatives to pads and tampons with plastic lining or packaging are reusable cotton pads, tampons with cardboard applicators, or internal silicone menstrual cups from brands like Mooncup. Though the latter may feel strange at first, this toxin-free, easy-to use and money-saving alternative is gradually winning mainstream support, and represents a real step forward in the battle to reduce waste.

#59

TOOTHPASTE TROUBLESHOOTING

Did you know that the average person will use around 389 tubes of toothpaste in their lifetime? As a result, millions of empty tubes are thrown away every year, but these squeezable toothpaste tubes are difficult to recycle and it's unusual for councils to include them as part of their collection schemes. A better alternative is the larger, pump-action toothpaste tube, which is made from a different type of plastic and typically easier to recycle. Making your own toothpaste, meanwhile, is a great way to skip all plastic waste, plus it's incredibly simple to do. Just blitz two tablespoons of bicarbonate of soda with four tablespoons coconut oil and store in a glass and aluminum screw-top jar.

#60

BRUSH WITH BAMBOO

Dentists recommend that you change your toothbrush every three months. If you follow this advice, you will have used 320 toothbrushes by the time you reach 80 years old! This part of our daily routine sees billions of plastic toothbrushes headed to landfills every year. Using an electric toothbrush with detachable heads around half the size of a normal toothbrush helps reduce the problem, but not completely. Why not go one step further and use plastic-free bamboo toothbrushes? These novel brushes are totally biodegradable and can be simply chucked onto your compost heap. Watch out for the nylon bristles, which do need to be pulled out before composting but can then be recycled. While you're at it, next time you need a new hairbrush or comb, skip plastic varieties and look out for eco wood or bamboo options with natural rubber or wooden bristles.

#61
DITCH DISPOSABLE RAZORS

This is a pretty easy choice that we can all make. Using endless disposable razors creates a huge amount of plastic waste. As well as the plastic handles, there are the blister packs they come in, which can only be recycled in some areas. Stainless steel razors, however, can be recycled, last longer and will also save you money in the long run. Plus, you can buy the refill blades in recyclable paper wraps – no plastic required.

#62
CAN COTTON BUDS

Cotton buds are largely made of plastic, thanks to their polypropylene stem. In fact, they are one of the top 10 items found on beaches by litter collection volunteers for the Marine Conservation Society. This is because people often wrongly flush them down the toilet and they end up passing through the sewage system and into the sea. However, the humble cotton bud can be deadly to any unfortunate marine life that ingest them. So ban buds from your bathroom now and instead buy one of the newer brands that now offer 100 per cent biodegradable organic cotton buds – usually made from bamboo sticks and soft cotton. The best ones can be simply thrown into your organic waste or compost bin.

#63
DIY BEAUTY PRODUCTS

The perfect way to save on plastic is to make your own beauty essentials. Once you've purchased the initial ingredients it's much cheaper, involves less plastic waste and you have the benefit of knowing there are no nasty chemicals hiding in your concoctions. If you're trying any of our recipes opposite you should also invest in a wholesale pack of glass jars with metal screw-top lids to keep your homemade products in. Or, even cheaper, simply sterilize some old condiment jars by washing them with soap and water then place them in a large pan of boiling water for 10 minutes, leaving to drain and air-dry on a clean tea towel.

Perfect pressies
Glass jars or homemade beauty products also make fantastic plastic-free presents. Buy some brown paper labels and write your own name and the product – in a fancy script, if you can! – adding the date they were handmade. It's important to remember that without the chemical preservatives that are found in shop-bought beauty items, homemade beauty products are at risk of growing bacteria and so won't last as long. As a rule, however, anything that only contains oils and no water – as with all the products – won't grow mould and can therefore be kept longer. Store in a cool, dark place and stop using if they ever start to smell funny.

Magic moisturizer

This can be used on the face and body for softer skin.

Ingredients

12 tablespoons shea butter (find online at beauty wholesalers or in health food shops)
3 tablespoons of any plant oil (sweet almond or olive oil work well)
1 tablespoon argan oil (optional)
3 drops chamomile essential oil
1 drop lavender essential oil

To make: Mix all the ingredients together by hand, or for a smoother consistency whiz in a clean blender. Decant into a glass screw-top jar.

Lovely lip balm

Perfect for soothing and protecting dry lips.

Ingredients

1½ teaspoons beeswax (available online or from health shops)
2 teaspoons shea butter
2 teaspoons extra virgin olive oil
3 drops lavender oil, or any essential oil of your choice

To make: Melt the beeswax and shea butter slowly in a metal bowl over a saucepan containing about 5 cm (2 in) of boiling water. Turn off the heat and add the olive oil and essential oil. Stir well and quickly, while mixture is still on the stove, so it doesn't solidify. Pour the mixture into small glass pots with screw-top lids. Leave to cool down before using.

Beautiful body scrub

A natural way to slough off dead skin cells.

Ingredients

16 tablespoons (1 cup) of organic coconut oil

1 tablespoon of sweet almond oil

6 tablespoons of coarse sea salt (the Himalayan pink variety looks pretty and contains skin-friendly minerals)

½ teaspoon of vanilla extract

Seeds from 5 cardamom pods

To make: Using a pestle and mortar, crush your cardamom seeds until a fine texture. Then add the coconut oil, sweet almond oil and vanilla and mix until creamy. Finally stir in the salt and transfer to a jar ready to use.

#64

CUT BACK ON DETERGENT BOTTLES

One easy way to reduce packaging is to seek out your nearest large health food store – they should offer refills of eco-friendly brands like Ecover or Method. There's also a new and innovative company called Splosh that sends highly concentrated liquid in returnable and reusable plastic pouches. This means the pouches last a lot longer, as you add water at home, but also you never have to throw them away – you simply return them in the cardboard-envelopes they come in.

Conventional powdered laundry soap comes in cardboard boxes with a plastic lining and usually include plastic scoops. To avoid plastic altogether, try using pure soap flakes in biodegradable packaging (from supermarkets) or soap nuts. These dried fruits contain a natural soap that lathers up when in contact with water and are a great, all-green way to wash clothes. You can find soap nuts in organic stores or online.

#65

IMPROVE YOUR
MULTI-TASKING SKILLS

Keep cleaning simple. Instead of buying lots of different products for different cleaning jobs, opt for multi-purpose cleaners that can do the lot. For example, just one bottle of multi-purpose cleaner can be used on kitchen work surfaces, the hob, your bath, sink and shower. This will save you lots of cupboard space too.

#66

MAKE YOUR DISHWASHER
PLASTIC FREE

Dishwasher tablets that come individually wrapped in plastic create more waste than a box of loose powder. Think about your choices and have a look at what is left to be disposed of after use. Some brands, such as Ecoleaf, offer eco-friendly dishwasher tablets with a soluble wrapper made from plant derived ingredients that are biodegradable. They also come in a plastic-free recyclable cardboard box.

DIY CLEANING PRODUCTS

Not only are homemade solutions less toxic and more cost-effective, you'll eliminate the need for multiple plastic bottles of brand-name cleaners. Best of all, making a good cleaning solution is much easier than you think.

#67
TRY VERSATILE VINEGAR

White vinegar diluted one part with three parts warm water makes a cheap and effective natural surface cleaner. Be sure to buy the vinegar in a glass bottle and decant into an old cleaning bottle spray. This mixture also works for keeping limescale at bay on taps, tiles, sinks and baths. To remove limescale from kettles, just fill with a solution of one-part water to one-part white vinegar and leave overnight. In the morning, the limescale will come off easily – but remember to rinse thoroughly to remove the taste. You can also do the same with shower-heads. Finally, vinegar solution also makes for a great plastic-free toilet cleaner. Leave a good glug in the bowl overnight and scrub with a wooden toilet brush with natural bristles the next day.

#68
SPARKLE WITH SODA

Bicarbonate of soda is a powerful natural deodorizer, which is great for removing smells from fridges, carpets and upholstery. For fridges, just leave a shallow bowl of bicarbonate of soda on one of the shelves. For soft furnishings, sprinkle onto the area and leave for a few hours, then suck up using the small nozzle on your vacuum cleaner. A scouring paste made from half bicarbonate of soda and half water is also great for removing stains from worktops, sinks, cookers and saucepans. Best of all, bicarbonate of soda can be bought and stored in recyclable cardboard boxes – no plastic required.

#69
LEMON JUICE IS A MUST

The citric acid contained in lemons is a natural bleaching agent. Use it to remove stains from chopping boards by rubbing them with fresh lemon and leave overnight. Lemon juice is also effective at removing rust stains from metal objects or clothing and adding half a capful into your wash will brighten whites.

#70

SWITCH TO REUSABLE CLEANING CLOTHS

If you get through a large number of non-recyclable washing-up sponges and cloths in your quest for cleanliness, this is an easy area to clean up your act. A silicone dish scrubber is a great alternative to plastic, not least because it's washable and reusable, which means it's also more cost-effective. Plus, research shows the material is less of a breeding ground for bacteria than traditional sponges, so you're improving your kitchen hygiene too.

If you need something with more scrubbing power, go for copper scourers, which are reusable, or a natural loofah scrubber which is completely biodegradable and can be used for anything from scrubbing pots and pans to cleaning grimy bathrooms. Once you've finished with loofahs, they can safely go in the compost. Finally, for wiping and polishing tasks, simply swap to cotton dishcloths or microfibre e-cloths, which can survive multiple washing machine cycles and will last for years.

#71
BIN LINERS

If you're composting your food waste and recycling the remainder, there's no real reason to use a single use plastic bag bin liner – just leave the bin naked and simply give it a good rinse each time you empty it. Or you could try lining it with old newspaper to soak up any bin juice. Don't make the mistake of reusing plastic shopping bags as kitchen bin liners – this may seem like smart repurposing but each bag is still very much destined for landfill.

#72
SPRAY, DON'T PLUG!

If you use air fresheners then steer clear of the plug-in ones made from hard, non-recyclable plastic that often come in blister packs – these packs are not selected for recycling by councils in many parts of the UK. Opt instead for pump-spray air fresheners. Or, for a more natural option, try using an oil burner to burn a few drops of your favourite essential oil.

Our current love affair with cheap, fast fashion is disastrous for our planet. Because if there is one thing that "retail therapy" does not fix, it's the massive pollution caused by an industry hooked on synthetic materials.

#73

SHOP LESS, SHOP NATURAL

Buying fewer, better-quality clothes is a good way to reduce plastic pollution. Firstly, because high-quality fabrics are more likely to be natural fibres such as cotton or wool, rather than synthetic plastic-containing fabrics such as nylon or polyester. Good-quality clothes also tend to be kept for longer and are easier to recycle, while cheaper garments are more likely to end up at best at the charity shop or at worst in a landfill. Some synthetic fabrics are recyclable but this tends to be an expensive process.

So before you make your next fashion purchase, ask yourself the following:

1. Is this a good-quality piece that will last a long time?
2. Will I still want to wear this in two years?
3. Do I have something already I can match it with?

#74
AVOID SYNTHETIC FABRICS

A lot of plastic pollution that flows into the sea comes from microfibres – the tiny fibres that wash out of clothes made from synthetic materials such as polyester, nylon, acrylic and Lycra. So it makes sense to commit to only buying natural fabrics such as cotton, silk and bamboo whenever possible. Tencel (also known as Lyocell), a fabric made from the natural cellulose fibres found in eucalyptus wood pulp, is another great choice as it doesn't shed and is biodegradable. If you already have a lot of synthetics, there are now products aimed at counteracting the shedding of these fibres. For example, Guppy Friend filter bags go into your washing machine and trap microfibres to prevent them from getting into the water system.

#75
CLOTHES HANGER CULL

Disposable plastic hangers tend to be made from a mixture of plastic and metal, meaning they're difficult to recycle, which is why millions end up in landfills every year. Start refusing to take home "free" plastic coat hangers when shopping and only buy wooden or stainless steel ones from now on. Charity shops will usually take old hangers to reuse, as will some dry cleaners. A few big supermarkets will now accept plastic coat hangers for recycling – confirm with your local store first. You could also try offering a batch of hangers on your local Freecycle site, where many unwanted items are quickly collected.

LOW-PLASTIC PARENTHOOD

A study by ChannelMum.com in 2018 found that nearly 90 per cent of parents admitted their plastic use had soared after having children. And it's easy to see why: the average single person throws away about 329 plastic items a year, while a family of four tosses out an incredible 2,764 plastic items per year. Thankfully, with a few simple lifestyle changes, it is possible to be a good parent and reduce your plastic use at the same time.

#76

SAY NO TO DISPOSABLE NAPPIES

With newborns going through six to 12 nappies a day, when it comes to reducing plastic waste, ditching disposable nappies is a no-brainer. The in-between measure is to use organic, biodegradable nappies made from natural fibres such as bamboo instead of the plastic used in standard nappies. Bear in mind bamboo nappies will still end up in a landfill, but the better biodegradable ones do promise to decompose in just two to three years – compared to some 200–500 years with standard nappies. But your greenest bet is to stick with reusable cloth nappies fixed with an old-fashioned safety pin. Insert washable, reusable liners to increase absorbency and reduce mess, or try biodegradable, flushable liners.

#77

USE WASHCLOTHS OVER WIPES

So called "baby wipes" have become an almost indispensable all-purpose cleaning tool for new parents, but as we've seen earlier in this book, disposable wipes can't be recycled and so generate a huge amount of landfill waste. This means that anyone aiming to be plastic free has no other option than to skip the wipes and get back to basics. And all you really need are damp flannels to keep your baby's bottom clean and fresh. Simply use warm water and mild soap.

#78

TRY BREASTFEEDING, IF POSSIBLE

Not only is breastfeeding healthy for your baby, it's also perfectly plastic free because it generates absolutely no waste. You'll avoid all the packaging that formula milk comes in, as well as the normally plastic bottles and sterilization equipment. All of which means you'll also save a lot of money too. But if you are bottle feeding, it's now possible to buy baby bottles made from toughened glass and teats made of natural rubber.

#79
BATCH-COOK BABY FOOD

They may be handy but those on-the-go foil food pouches, containing
pureed fruit and veg, are non-recyclable and one of the worst
offenders when it comes to plastic pollution. Glass jars with metal
screw tops are much more eco-friendly, but better still – and cheaper
– is making your own baby food. Make large batches, store in
reusable containers, or freeze in stainless steel ice-cube trays.

#80
PICK PLASTIC-FREE SKIN CARE

Nearly all baby lotions come in plastic packaging. The good news
is, you really don't need anything special to keep your baby clean. In
fact, using fewer products is probably better for your baby's skin as
you won't irritate it or strip away the natural moisture. So stick with a
mild soap bought package-free at your local health food store. You
can moisturize and treat nappy rash with coconut oil, which can be
bought in glass jars.

#81

FORGET FANCY GADGETS

As anyone with more than one child will tell any new parent, all those plastic-laden gadgets aimed at first-timers – from music-playing swing chairs, fancy nappy bins, movement sensors and wipe warmers – are completely unnecessary. They don't make parenting easier, plus they create a huge amount of plastic waste. Keep it simple and cost-effective by asking around experienced parents to create a hitlist of the items you really need — and those you can safely ignore. Also, be on the lookout for what you can grab second hand rather than new.

#82
TURN DOWN FREE PLASTIC

When children get a little older, it's a good idea to establish a firm "no" position to all those "free" plastic toys that come with fast food and some food products. Most of this stuff is destined straight for the bin and then the dreaded landfill anyway. And while refusing sweets with toys might make your children temporarily cross, consistency is key and you can always find alternative treats. Plus, exercising your power as a consumer will help big brands get the message on slashing plastic use.

#83
CLEANER CLEAN-UP OPERATION

Whether it's picking up after your dog on a walk or cleaning out your cat's litter tray, plastic bags are often used to collect and dispose of pet waste. And even if you're averaging a conservative two plastic bags a day, that's over 100 bags ending up in landfills every year. The simple answer to this messy problem is to swap to biodegradable bags. While they will still take some time to break down in an oxygen-starved landfill, they're a far more eco-friendly alternative and won't end up making their way into the oceans and polluting them. When it comes to cats, choose biodegradable litter options, such as old newspapers or wood shavings.

#84
GO GREEN WITH TOYS

They keep your pet entertained and physically fit, but, unfortunately, many dog and cat toys are manufactured with cheap plastic that can't be recycled. Look instead for toys made from alternative materials such as canvas, natural rubber or cotton. Rope pulls and cardboard cat scratching posts are great examples of toys made from recycled material that are also recyclable themselves. And instead of just throwing out any plastic items that your pet no longer needs, see if you can donate them to your nearest animal rescue centre, where they will be gratefully received.

#85
THINK ABOUT FOOD

Pet food, just like human food, has the potential to introduce a huge amount of plastic waste into our lives. For starters, choosing stainless steel or ceramic food and water bowls over plastic is the smart move. When it comes to buying food itself, the main varieties to ditch are the individual-portion foil pouches, which are lined with plastic and almost impossible to recycle. Cans from canned pet food are easy to recycle once cleaned out, as are the paper bags or cardboard boxes typically used to house dried food. Try to buy in bulk and store in glass or stainless steel pet food canisters, such as the ones made by luxury bin company Simple Human.

10 EASY
UPCYCLING
PLASTIC
PROJECTS

The more plastic you can find another use for around your home and garden, the less chance it will wind up stuck in a landfill for several hundred years or polluting our oceans. Here are some simple ideas to get you started.

#86
SELF-WATERING BOTTLE PLANTERS

These fab indoor plant holders are not only a perfect way to reuse large plastic bottles, they're also handy for those of us who forget to water plants regularly too!

What you'll need: tape measure, three 2-litre bottles, masking tape, scissors, acrylic paint, paintbrush, one nail, a hammer, large wool needle and twine or wool, potting compost and three seedlings.

To make: First measure around 12 cm (4 $^1/_2$ in) up from the bottom of your water bottle, and cut around it with scissors. Then wrap a piece of masking tape around the removed top part of the bottle and paint it any colour you like. Leave to dry. Next, carefully hammer the nail through the centre of the bottle's lid to make a hole. Thread your needle with a 25 cm (10 in) piece of twine or wool and push it through the hole, leaving about 12 cm (4 $^1/_2$ in) of yarn on both sides of the lid. Fill the top half of your bottle with potting compost. Plant your seedlings into the soil. Fill the bottom half of the bottle with water. The yarn acts as a wick and the plants will take the water as they need it, while the clear bottles help you to spot when the water needs refilling.

#87
OUTDOOR LOTUS
FLOWER CANDLE HOLDERS

Nobody will believe these beautiful, flower-shaped candle holders are made from old milk bottles and not from a fancy garden shop.

What you'll need: Two clean 4-litre (1 gallon) plastic milk bottles, scrap card for templates, scissors, clear silicone glue, two battery-powered tea lights.

To make: The first step is to make three different-sized templates to draw your petals around. To create the open flower effect, it's good to have around eight small petals (around 6 cm (2 ½ in) long) for the centre, followed by six medium petals (8 cm (3 in)) and then six large (10 cm (4 in)) for the outside.

Cut out your petals from the milk bottle, as well as a circular centrepiece – draw around a tea light for this. Now glue everything together. Start with the circle and stick the smallest petals first, going around in a floral shape. Wait 10 minutes so the glue can set. Then attach the medium-sized petals, followed by the large petals. Turn upside down to dry, placing the tea light in the centre afterward.

#88
LOTTA BOTTLE BIRD FEEDER

This plastic bottle bird feeder and perch simply refills through the cap of the bottle – and has fab wooden spoon perches so your feathered friends can easily dine.

What you'll need: A craft knife, two old wooden spoons, screw-in hook for hanging, paintbrush, empty 2-litre (half US gallon) plastic bottle and lid, waterproof paint for decoration and birdseed.

To make: First, you need to carefully cut four holes, using a craft knife, so you can thread your wooden spoons all the way through the bottle – with the handle poking out of one side and the spoon part on the other. One spoon can go through the higher part of the bottle, and the other through the lower. The hole at the spoon end should be bigger than the handle and quite loose so that seed can spill through onto the spoon and birds can perch and feed, with the hole at the handle end a tighter fit to hold it in place.

Next, screw the hook into the bottle lid. Finally, paint some fun swirls or patterns of your choice onto the feeder and spoon ledges to make it look pretty – fill, hang in a tree and watch the birds tuck in.

#89
FAIRY LIGHTS LANTERN

Give a water or cola bottle a new purpose by converting it into a stylish lantern with a geometric pattern.

What you'll need: A 2-litre water or cola bottle, scissors, a string of battery powered LED fairy lights, pencil, cardboard for a template, clear glue and some sheets of white paper.

Warning: Only use fairy lights with LED bulbs, otherwise the lantern may overheat, melt the plastic and become dangerous.

To make: Cut off the neck of the bottle so you have a handy open container. Then add in your string of LED lights. Next, cut a cardboard template of your chosen geometric shape – diamonds or hexagons work well – and trace a repeated pattern using a pencil across your sheet of paper – either going vertically or horizontally all over the paper. Cut your shapes out. Wrap and stick a plain sheet of paper around the bottle, ensuring it's at least 6 cm (2 $^1/_2$ in) above the top of the bottle so you won't see it. Then wrap and stick your cut-out sheet on top – these two layers will allow the fairy lights to twinkle through the pattern without seeing the bottle behind.

#90
RECYCLED WIND CHIMES

Teach your children the importance of upcycling with this
fun wind chime.

What you'll need: Scissors, a 2-litre bottle (half US gallon), paintbrush,
colourful acrylic paints, yarn or string made from waterproof material,
lots of old chunky beads and/or chopped up old plastic drinking
straws, four large metal buttons, a hole punch, clear varnish and a
metal hook for hanging.

To make: Cut off the tapered, top portion of the plastic bottle. Paint
the bottle in bold, bright colours of your choice. When the paint is
dry, punch four evenly spaced holes around the bottom of the bottle.
A coat of clear varnish is optional but will give the wind chime some
shine and help protect it from the elements. String four equal length
pieces of yarn (about 15 cm (6 in) with lots of colourful beads and
small sections of straws, aiming to put one metal button in about the
middle of each, for weight and sound. Leave 6 cm (2 $^1/_2$ in) of space
at the top of each strand, then slip each one through a punched hole,
and knot it in place. Screw a metal hook into the bottom of the bottle
and hang your wind chime somewhere it will catch the breeze.

#91
MOBILE PHONE HOLDER

This rather cunning idea keeps your mobile safe so you can't misplace it at home – and best of all, it costs next to nothing.

What you'll need: One empty, rinsed-out plastic beauty bottle – body lotion or shampoo with an oval base will work well, and you should measure it against your mobile phone to ensure it isn't too big or too small. Also scissors, sandpaper, paintbrush, acrylic paint or fabric scraps and glue.

To make: Cut in a straight line around the front and back of the bottle at a height that will allow your mobile to sit above the top by about a third of its height. You might also want to make a small hole for a power lead to slip through. Use some sandpaper to smooth any rough edges. Then either paint it the colour of your choice or stick on colourful, old fabric scraps with glue to cover the outside completely. Wait for it to dry and, hey presto, you have a standing mobile holder to keep your phone from getting lost or to store it neatly as it charges.

#92
RAISED PATIO FLOWER BEDS

Impossible-to-recycle, moulded polystyrene pieces can make excellent DIY raised beds for garden flowers.

What you'll need: Large, deep, moulded polystyrene pieces – the type that arrive in big boxes of electrical appliances or disposable cool boxes – paintbrush, terracotta coloured acrylic paint, craft knife, potting compost and plants of your choice.

To make: Paint the polystyrene troughs outside, and from the top to about halfway down inside. You can choose any colour you like, but a terracotta shade will add a lovely rustic clay-brick feel. Leave to dry. The polystyrene may come with drainage holes as part of the manufacturing process, but if not, carefully use a craft knife to make your own. Then simply add potting compost and some lovely bright patio flowers such as geraniums, petunias or hydrangeas. Water and leave to flourish.

#93
COLOURFUL OUTDOOR BUNTING

Polystyrene plates that have been used at parties often just get chucked out, only to end up in a landfill. But washed and painted, they can be used to make beautiful, weatherproof party bunting.

What you'll need: 10 or so used but washed polystyrene plates, scissors, paintbrush, garden twine, thick sewing needle, acrylic paints.

To make: Cut the plates into bunting-sized triangles, fitting in as many triangles per plate as possible. Then paint both sides in a variety of bright colours, picking any pattern or colour theme you fancy. Leave to dry, then paint over with white polka-dot splodges. Once completely dry, pierce holes in the triangles, thread onto some garden twine and hang around the garden.

#94
MAKE-UP ORGANIZER

Streamline your beauty pencils, lipsticks and brushes by reusing colourful old spray bottles, which often can't be easily recycled.

What you'll need: Two or three clean plastic spray bottles, ideally in different colours, rubber bands, permanent marker or Sharpie, scissors and a regular iron.

To make: Place a rubber band around the plastic bottle at the height you want to make your pot. Use the rubber band as a guide to draw a straight line all the way around the bottle and then cut around the bottle carefully. Turn the iron on high and very carefully, melt the cut edge of the plastic bottle by holding it against the iron. Only leave it on the iron for about five seconds – the rough edges will fold in on themselves, creating a smooth and rounded edge. Leave to cool, then repeat with as many bottles as you need to finally organize that make-up!

#95
UPCYCLED WATERING CAN

Rescue your empty laundry detergent bottle from a miserable life in a landfill by turning it into a pretty watering can.

What you'll need: One large, empty laundry detergent bottle with screw cap, paintbrush, acrylic paints, a sharp metal prong (such as a meat skewer) for making holes in the lids.

To make: Thoroughly rinse your bottle out with clean water, repeating several times to ensure no traces of detergent that might harm your plants remain. Remove the bottle label. Paint either the entire bottle or, if you like its original base colour, simply paint a pattern on top. For example, cheerful daisies or bumble bees. While it's drying, very carefully use a metal prong to make several small holes in the lid. Then voilà, water away.

#96
FIVE UPCYCLING QUICK WINS

----

1 Use smaller plastic bottles as cane toppers in your vegetable garden. As well as making the tops safer, they help keep birds away and can be used to support netting.

2 Tubs containing the likes of margarine and ice cream can be reused as useful dividers and organizers inside drawers and cupboards

3 Jars with plastic lids can be used to put refills of herbs and spices in, or to hold nails, screws and bolts, etc.

4 Get at least a second use out of old polystyrene bits and bobs as they're very handy for cushioning delicate items in a house move or for sending breakables through the post.

5 Use the top half of a plastic 2-litre (half US gallon) drinks bottle as a makeshift plunger next time your sink is bunged up, to avoid having to use harsh drain cleaner or call out a pricey plumber.

RESPONSIBLE RECYCLING

Using as little plastic as possible is a vital and significant step everyone can make in reducing the enormous amount of plastic pollution in the environment. But with worldwide plastic consumption now so huge, and many plastic alternatives too prohibitively expensive to be used by all, combining this approach with effective recycling – the only real way to tackle the problem head-on.

In fact, many environmental experts agree that the biggest problem with plastic use is not the sheer scale of it, but how little heed we pay to recycling the substance in all its forms. Despite concerted efforts around the world to make plastic recycling more mainstream and more accessible, we're still not doing enough. Read on to learn how you can become a better recycler.

#97
FIND OUT WHAT YOU CAN RECYCLE

Different areas around the country have different rules when it comes to what they can and can't recycle, so the first step is to check on your local council website to find out what exactly you can recycle via home collection. You may be able to take other items to a recycling drop-off point, so check your nearest location for this. Then, use the guidelines in this chapter to understand how to decode plastic packaging labels, and know at a glance if any item can be recycled and how.

#98
MAKE IT EASIER ON YOURSELF

Develop the habits of a recycler. For example, most jars and yogurt pots need a clean before they can be recycled, so get used to leaving them to soak in the sink when they're finished – or putting them through the dishwasher with the rest of your wash. And keep your recycling bin next to the main bin so you can take out the rubbish and recycling at the same time each week.

#99
RECYCLE BATHROOM WASTE TOO

This may seem obvious, but, according to the Recycle Now campaign, only 50 per cent of packaging is recycled in the bathroom compared to nearly 90 per cent in the kitchen. Some of this difference is just down to the inconvenience factor, so you could consider adding a separate recycling bin in your bathroom. Another reason more bathroom items are thrown in the bin is due to confusion over what can and can't be recycled. However, you can normally recycle most common items including your empty shampoo, conditioner, shower gel and moisturizer bottles, aerosols for deodorant and shaving foam and bathroom cleaning bottles.

CAN I RECYCLE ALL PLASTIC?

You might assume that if it's possible to recycle one type of plastic, you should be able to recycle anything made from plastic. But in practice it's a bit trickier. There are more than 50 different types of plastic, making it more difficult to sort and reprocess than other recyclable materials. Nearly all types of plastic can be recycled in theory, but the extent to which they actually are depends on factors such as cost and whether the right sorting and recycling technology is available in the area you live.

So, while pretty much everywhere can – and does – recycle plastic bottles, other plastics are more problematic. One example is the black plastic food trays used in a lot of supermarket packaging – most recycling companies will not collect them because their dark colour makes them invisible to the sorting machine scanners at the recycling plant. Companies are currently looking at developing new technology to try and overcome this problem but an effective, widespread solution is still some time away.

Further confusing everyday food recycling is that while some yogurt pots are made from polyethylene terephthalate – the same recyclable material that is used for plastic bottles – other yogurt pots are made from polystyrene, which is not accepted in most domestic recycling collections. Plus, many butter and margarine tubs look recyclable but are in fact made from a mixture of plastics, which can only be broken down by technology not readily available in the UK. This means they can only be shipped abroad for recycling.

If all this sounds like a confusing minefield, thankfully, there is at least an easy number method to help you decode all your domestic plastics.

THE SEVEN GRADES OF PLASTIC

Have you ever seen the little triangle made of arrows and containing a number on the bottom of a plastic item? This is what's known as its plastic grade. The system, devised in America, separates plastics into seven grades depending on what type of plastic they're made from. And the grades you can pop in your home recycling bin depend entirely on your local council and which they accept. This information is available on your local council website, so knowing to look for the number makes it easy to work out which plastics are safe to recycle – and which you can't. To help you further, here's a guide to what each number grade means.

PET

1. POLYETHYLENE TEREPHTHALATE (PET)

The most commonly used plastics are the ones with a triangle that contains a number 1 and are made from PET. This includes nearly all plastic drinks bottles. It's a highly recyclable material and 94 per cent of UK councils will now collect PET plastic bottles either from your doorstep or from recycling centres. Indeed, according to the UK Household Plastics Collection Survey 2016, almost 60 per cent of PET plastics are being collected for recycling from households. Which is not bad, but could be better.

What can it be used for? Plenty. PET bottles can be recycled and made back into bottles for soft drinks – or transformed completely into carpets, bags, or thermal stuffing for coats.

HDPE

2. HIGH-DENSITY POLYETHYLENE (HDPE)

This is a much thicker, tougher sort of plastic that is used for bottles containing products such as milk, fruit juice, shampoo and cleaning fluids. HDPE is 100 per cent recyclable and bottles made from it are collected by 92 per cent of councils, with 79 per cent of these bottles recycled here in the UK.

What can it be used for? Quite a lot actually. It can be recycled into garden furniture, litter bins, pipes, crates and fencing.

PVC

3. POLYVINYL CHLORIDE (PVC)

PVC can be rigid or flexible. In its rigid state, it is found in window frames, drain pipes and bank cards. The flexible version is used to make clingfilm, medicine blister packs, garden furniture, plastic toys and insulation for electrical wiring. It can also be used as a leather substitute in clothes and shoes. However, PVC in any form is not generally collected from households for recycling.

What can it be used for? Not a great deal. Despite its obvious versatility, PVC is rarely recycled and can actually be dangerous, if ingested. If it is recycled, it's commonly reduced to its component chemicals and turned into more PVC or used for industrial-grade items such as flooring. Thankfully, PVC use in packaging is in decline.

4

LDPE

4. LOW-DENSITY POLYETHYLENE (LDPE)

Plastic bags and six-pack beer rings, clingfilm, sandwich bags and squeezable bottles are all made from LDPE. Many of these items are the most dangerous and most polluting of all common plastic products – turning up in the oceans, where they cause havoc to the ecosystem. Again, LDPE is commonly not collected from households for recycling.

What can it be used for? Grade 4 plastics can be reformed into lumber (a plastic wood replacement) and then built into a variety of objects. Despite this usefulness, they're currently rarely recycled – just 5 per cent of what's produced. Carrier bags are collected by some supermarkets and recycled for low-grade uses such as bin bags.

5

PP

5. POLYPROPYLENE (PP)

Polypropylene has a high softening point, so it is often used for containers that will house hot drinks, soups, takeaway containers, margarine tubs, yogurt pots, drinking straws and medicine bottles. It's another material that contributes hugely to plastic pollution and is one of the most common types found in the ocean.

What can it be used for? PP can be recycled into a few very specific items, such as ice scrapers, battery cables and rakes. However, in most areas, Grade 5 plastics are not currently recycled, which means that only 1 per cent of all PP gets recycled.

6

PS

6. POLYSTYRENE (PS)

Famously difficult to recycle, PS is used in packaging, polystyrene takeaway cups and food boxes. Recycling Grade 6 plastics is very expensive because it uses a lot of energy, so it is rarely done. Unfortunately, polystyrene is now the leading cause of plastic pollution in the oceans. Thankfully, there are more and more alternatives to Grade 6 plastics being introduced, such as biodegradable food boxes and coffee cups.

What can it be used for? Not much, with the only common secondary use for polystyrene being to shred it into tiny balls for cavity wall insulation.

7

OTHER

7. EVERYTHING ELSE

Basically, a hotchpotch group of plastics that don't fit into any of the other six grades. Some common plastics that fall into this group are polylactide – used in 3D printing – and polycarbonate, which is widely used in roofing. Items made from a blend of plastics also fall into this category. These types of plastic are very hard to recycle due to the wide range of chemicals used in their manufacture.

What can it be used for? Not a lot. The fact that this category contains a bit of everything means that there is no one-size-fits-all solution to recycling plastics stamped with a number 7. With sufficient resources, some types can be turned into "plastic lumber", which can then be used in the construction industry.

#100
SEE IT, SORT IT!

The key to recycling properly is getting to know how common household items fit into the Grade 1 to 7 plastic system, and which grades your local kerbside collection will take away. Unfortunately, for most places in the UK, it's usually only Grades 1 and 2 plastics that are regularly collected and recycled.

If your local authority doesn't collect certain types of plastic, it's important that they don't end up in your recycling bin. The collection staff probably won't know – or be able to see at a glance – if your bin contains items that can't be recycled, so the unwanted items will only be discovered at the recycling plant. At this point, the non-recyclable plastic will have taken up unnecessary space on collection vehicles and will cost extra money to be separated from the other plastics and disposed of. To make matters worse, if the overall levels of contamination in a recycling batch are deemed too high because it contains too many non-recyclable pieces of plastic, there's a strong chance the whole lot will end up in landfill anyway. Which means after a lot of time, money and effort, we're just back to square one.

Your best bet with Grades 3 to 7 is to check your local council website if you're not sure and lobby them to change their policy if they currently collect only Grades 1 and 2. Remember, positive people power really can change the world!

STOCKISTS

----

www.zero-waste-club.com

   Organic, plastic-free grocery delivery.

www.theplasticfreeshop.co.uk

   Plastic-free alternatives to everyday products.

www.wearthlondon.com

   Beauty products, food containers and homeware.

www.ecco-verde.co.uk

   Natural make-up and skincare with a plastic-free packaged range.

www.anythingbutplastic.co.uk

   Household products, storage, beauty and cleaning products.

packagefreeshop.com

   Stylish plastic-free homeware, travel, office and personal products.

wildminimalist.com

   Zero-waste starter kits to begin the plastic-free journey.

oneplanetzero.com

   Tableware, baby care and bamboo sunglasses and watches.

sinplastico.com

   Spanish website with alternatives to everyday products.

sans-bpa.com

   French website for plastic-free items for the kitchen, bathroom and office.

econea.cz

   Czech website stocking candles, textiles, menstruation products and
   household products.

laguna-onlineshop.de

   Everything from camping equipment to smartphone sleeves.

www.monomeer.de

   German site stocking deodorant, razors, soaps, food wraps and glass straws.

sapontina.gr

Based in Greece, lifestyle products and food storage.

www.ecomondo.nl

Avocado huggers, tumblers, growkits and solar lamps, based in Netherlands.

thesourcebulkfoods.com.au

With branches in Australia, New Zealand and the UK. Bulk-buy grains, nuts, rice, flour, seeds, pasta, honey, oil and more.

www.floraandfauna.com.au

Household, make-up, dental, clothes and jewellery.

www.planetorganic.com

Stores around London selling bulk and plastic-free packaged items.

www.thecleankilo.co.uk

The UK's largest zero-waste supermarket, based in Birmingham.

www.harmlessstore.co.uk

The UK's smallest zero-waste store, with fish counter, vegetables and a bar.

ethicalsuperstore.com

Bamboo and corn-starch plates and coffee cups.

www.comptoir-des-savonniers-paris.fr

Unpackaged handmade soaps from Paris.

www.moncharbon.com

Activated charcoal for water filtration. Based in France.

halo.coffee

Compostible coffee cups.

sodastream.co.uk

Make your own carbonated drinks.

INDEX